MY MOST SINCERE APUGLOGIES

_____

_____

_____

_____

I'M SORRY FOR **EVERYTHING** I DON'T REMEMBER FROM LAST NIGHT.

MY MOST SINCERE APOLOGIES

_____

_____

_____

_____

I'M SORRY
I FORGOT

A) YOUR BIRTHDAY
B) OUR ANNIVERSARY
C) VALENTINE'S DAY
D) ALL OF THE ABOVE

MY MOST SINCERE APUGLOGIES

_____

_____

_____

_____

I AM SO DOGGONE EMBARRASSED.

MY MOST SINCERE APUGLOGIES

APOLOGIES ABOUT
THE HOLIDAYS
(IN ADVANCE).

MY MOST SINCERE APUGLOGIES

_____

_____

_____

_____

SORRY I ATE ALL YOUR _____.

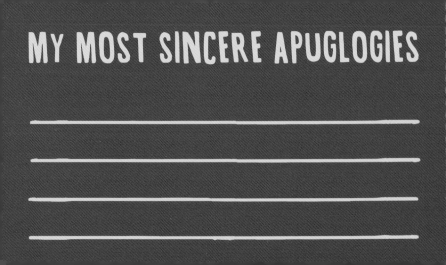

MY MOST SINCERE APUGLOGIES

THIS GOT OUT OF CONTROL FAST. (SORRY.)

MY MOST SINCERE APUGLOGIES

_____

_____

_____

_____

OOOO
OOOOOOO
OOOOOPPPP
PPPSSSSSSSS
SSSSSSS...

MY MOST SINCERE APUGLOGIES

_____

_____

_____

_____

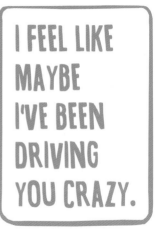

I FEEL LIKE
MAYBE
I'VE BEEN
DRIVING
YOU CRAZY.

MY MOST SINCERE APUGLOGIES

_____

_____

_____

_____

I MESSED UP AND IT'S COLD OUT HERE.

MY MOST SINCERE APUGLOGIES

_____

_____

_____

_____

SORRY I LET THINGS GET SO HEAVY.

MY MOST SINCERE APUGLOGIES

_____

_____

_____

_____

I PROMISE I'LL ALWAYS HAVE YOUR BACK FROM NOW ON.

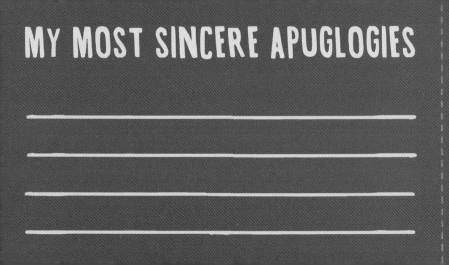

MY MOST SINCERE APUGLOGIES

_____

_____

_____

_____

YOU'VE SAVED MY LIFE.

MY MOST SINCERE APUGLOGIES

_____

_____

_____

_____

THIS HAS NOT
BEEN MY BEST
MOMENT.

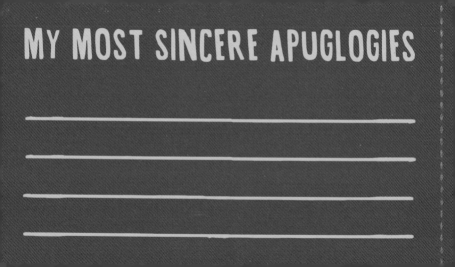

I'VE MADE A TERRIBLE MISTAKE.

MY MOST SINCERE APUGLOGIES

_____

_____

_____

_____

I OWE YOU
A REALLY
HUGE PARTY.

MY MOST SINCERE APUGLOGIES

_____

_____

_____

_____

I AM
THE
WORST.

MY MOST SINCERE APUGLOGIES

I'M SORRY
I WAS
SO TIRED...

MY MOST SINCERE APUGLOGIES

_____

_____

_____

_____

MY MOST SINCERE APUGLOGIES

_____

_____

_____

_____